Numbers and the Number System 3

Solutions

PUBLISHED BY THE PRESS SYNDICATE OF THE UNIVERSITY OF CAMBRIDGE
The Pitt Building, Trumpington Street, Cambridge, United Kingdom

CAMBRIDGE UNIVERSITY PRESS
The Edinburgh Building, Cambridge CB2 2RU, UK   http://www.cup.cam.ac.uk
40 West 20th Street, New York, NY 10011-4211, USA   http://www.cup.org
10 Stamford Road, Oakleigh, Melbourne 3166, Australia
Ruiz de Alarcón 13, 28014 Madrid, Spain

© Cambridge University Press 2000

First published 2000

Printed in the United Kingdom at the University Press, Cambridge

Typefaces Frutiger, Swift *System* QuarkXPress 4.03®

A catalogue record for this book is available from the British Library

ISBN 0 521 79821 3 paperback

General editors for Cambridge Mathematics Direct
Sandy Cowling, Jane Crowden, Andrew King, Jeanette Mumford

Writing team for *Numbers and the number system 3*
Mark Adams, Lynn Huggins-Cooper, Jeanette Mumford, Andrew King,
Marian Reynolds

The writers and publishers would like to thank the many schools and
individuals who trialled lessons for Cambridge Mathematics Direct.

NOTICE TO TEACHERS
The pages in this publication may be photocopied free of charge for
classroom use within the school or institution which purchases the publication.
The solutions and photocopies of them remain in the copyright of Cambridge
University Press and such photocopies may not be distributed or used in any
way outside the purchasing institution. Written permission is necessary if you wish to
store the material electronically.

Notes

Solutions to textbook and copymaster questions are listed under
the title of the lesson in the teacher's handbook. Lessons are
in the same order as in the teacher's handbook.

Solutions are written in different forms:
- Complete solutions are listed wherever it is useful.
- Facsimiles of completed copymasters are included where this
  is most helpful.
- For open-ended questions and investigations, the
  possibilities are indicated through examples.

You can learn most about children's misconceptions by marking
their work with them or discussing incorrect answers after marking.

Solutions may be photocopied (under the conditions detailed above).

Counting, properties of numbers and number sequences

N1.1 Counting collections

TB pages 5–6

B1   a   Tanya drew marks in groups of 10.
     b   She counted 63 jumps.

B2   a   Hassan counted 63 jumps.
     b   Hassan drew his marks in groups of 5.

B3   a ||||| ||||| ||||| ||||| ||||| ||||| ||||| |||

     b |||| |||| |||| |||| |||| |||| |||| |||| |||| |||| |||| |||| |||| |||

C1   The chart depends on the dice throws, but the tallies and totals should agree and there should be 6 of one number, and less than 6 of the rest.

N1.2 Ones and tens beyond one hundred

TB page 7

B1	a 59	b 126	c 264
B2	a 72	b 280	c 558
B3	a 80	b 175	c 450

B4   a and b

458			462	463	464		466

N1.3 Ones, tens and hundreds

TB page 8

B1   a   Counting on in 10s: 83, 93
     b   Counting back in 10s: 107, 97
     c   Counting back in 100s: 345, 245
     d   Counting on in 100s: 519, 619

B2   a   16, **36**, 56, 76, 96, 116, **136**, 156
     b   **115**, 125, 135, 145, 155, 165, **175**, 185
     c   53, **253**, 453, 653, **853**

B3   For example:
43, 143, 243, 343, 443, ... Add 100 each time.
789, 779, 769, 759, 749, ... Subtract 10 each time.

N2.1 Odds and evens

TB pages 9–10

A1   47 odd
     32 even
     90 even
     54 even
     65 odd
     79 odd

A2   a   46, 48, 50, 52
     b   28, 30, 32, 34, 36

A3   a   33, 35, 37, 39, 41
     b   69, 71, 73, 75, 77

B1   a   73, 61, 89
     b   91, 73, 101

B2   a   48, 70, 64
     b   58, 70, 100

B3   a   47, 49, 51, 53, **55**, **57**, **59**
     b   78, 76, 74, 72, **70**, **68**, **66**
     c   63, 65, 67, **69**, **71**, **73**
     d   25, 23, 21, **19**, **17**, **15**

CM 3

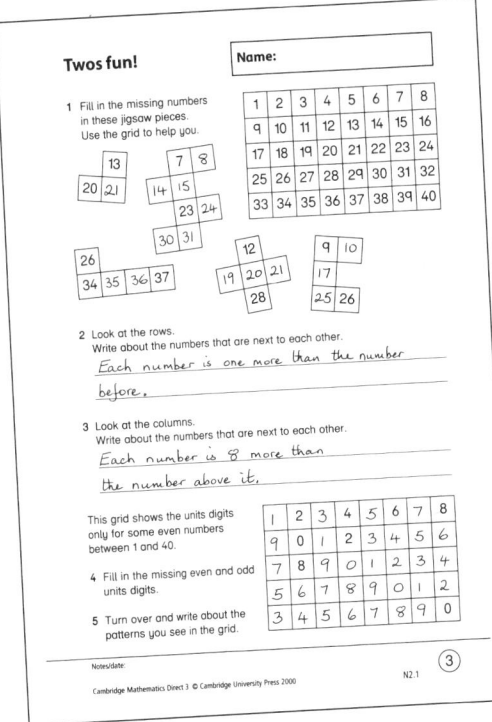

5   Numbers go up by 1 in the rows till they reach 9 and then go back to 0.
Numbers in the columns are part of the sequence 9, 7, 5, 3, 1, 9, 7, ... or the sequence 8, 6, 4, 2, 0, 8, 6, ...

N2.2 Adding and subtracting odds and evens

TB page 11

A1 12 + 6 = 18   12 + 4 = 16
    12 + 8 = 20   12 + 20 = 3
    6 + 4 = 10   6 + 8 = 14
    6 + 20 = 26   4 + 8 = 12
    4 + 20 = 24   8 + 20 = 28

A2 a 12 − 1 = 11   b 6 − 1 = 5
    c 4 − 1 = 3   d 8 − 1 = 7
    e 20 − 1 = 19

A3 For example
    a 11 − 3 = 8   b 5 − 5 = 0
    c 3 − 1 = 2   d 7 − 3 = 4
    e 19 − 11 = 8

A4 When I subtract an odd number from an odd number the answer is even.

B1 The cards can be in any order as long as the 4 even numbers are in the middle of the sides and the 5 odd numbers are at the corners and in the centre.

N2.3 What if?

TB page 12

A1 Total Dice score
    4   1 + 1 + 2
    6   1 + 1 + 4 or 1 + 2 + 3 or 2 + 2 + 2
    8   1 + 1 + 6 or 1 + 2 + 5 or 1 + 3 + 4
         or 2 + 2 + 4 or 2 + 3 + 3
    10   1 + 3 + 6 or 1 + 4 + 5 or 2 + 2 + 6
         or 2 + 3 + 5 or 2 + 4 + 4
         or 3 + 3 + 4
    12   1 + 5 + 6 or 2 + 4 + 6 or 2 + 5 + 5
         or 3 + 3 + 6 or 3 + 4 + 5
         or 4 + 4 + 4
    14   2 + 6 + 6 or 3 + 5 + 6 or 4 + 4 + 6
         or 4 + 5 + 5
    16   4 + 6 + 6 or 5 + 5 + 6
    18   6 + 6 + 6

B1 For example:
    4 = 1 + 1 + 1 + 1
    6 = 1 + 1 + 1 + 3
    8 = 1 + 1 + 3 + 3
    10 = 1 + 1 + 1 + 7
    12 = 1 + 1 + 1 + 9
    14 = 1 + 1 + 3 + 9
    16 = 1 + 1 + 5 + 9
    18 = 1 + 1 + 7 + 9
    20 = 1 + 1 + 9 + 9

B2 For example:
    4 = 1 + 1 + 1 + 1
    6 = 1 + 1 + 1 + 3
    8 = 1 + 1 + 3 + 3
    10 = 1 + 1 + 3 + 5
    12 = 1 + 1 + 5 + 5
    14 = 1 + 3 + 5 + 5
    16 = 3 + 3 + 5 + 5
    18 = 3 + 5 + 5 + 5
    20 = 5 + 5 + 5 + 5

CM 4

1

+	1	2	3	4	5	6
1	2		4		6	
2		4		6		8
3	4		6		8	
4		6		8		10
5	6		8		10	
6		8		10		12

2 2 → 1 + 1   4 → 2 + 2   6 → 3 + 3
   8 → 4 + 4   10 → 5 + 5   12 → 6 + 6

3 If I add 2 numbers that are the same, the answer is **even**.

CM 5

20 = 9 + 1 + 9 + 1 or
     9 + 1 + 7 + 3
     9 + 1 + 5 + 5
     9 + 3 + 3 + 5
     7 + 1 + 7 + 5
     7 + 3 + 7 + 3
     7 + 3 + 5 + 5
     5 + 5 + 5 + 5

If you include a 2-digit number there are more possibilities. For example:
20 = 11 + 1 + 1 + 7
     11 + 1 + 3 + 5

N3.1 Steps of 2, 3, 4 and 5

TB page 13

B1 a 18, 20, 22, 24, 26, 28
    b 5, 10, 15, 20, 25
    c 91, 81, 71, 61, 51, 41, 31
    d 35, 33, 31, 29, 27, 25
    e 6, 11, 16, 21, 26, 31, 36, 41

B2 a 3, 8, 13, 18, 23, 28
    b 20, 24, 28, 32, 36, 40, 44
    c 807, 707, 607, 507, 407, 307
    d 35, 31, 27, 23, 19, 15

B3 B1 a 30, 32, 34   b 30, 35, 40
    c 21, 11, 1   d 23, 21, 19
    e 46, 51, 56
    B2 a 33, 38, 43   b 48, 52, 56
    c 207, 107, 7   d 11, 7, 3

C1 For example:
    100, 95, 90, 85, 80, 75, ...
    2, 6, 10, 14, 18, 22, 26, 30, ...

N3.2 Making patterns by counting

CM 6

1   1, 4, 7, 10, 13, 16, 19, 22, 25
    The coloured squares are on diagonal lines.
2   3, 7, 11, 15, 19, 23
    The coloured squares are on different diagonal lines.
3   1, 3, 5, 7, 9, 11, 13, 15, 17, 19, 21, 23, 25
    The coloured squares make a check pattern.
4   4, 9, 14, 19, 24
    The coloured squares are all in 1 column.

CM 7

1   a 1, 5, 9, 13, 17, 21, 25, 29, 33
       37, 41, 45 are in the sequence.
    b 3, 8, 13, 18, 23, 28, 33
       38, 43, 48 are in the sequence.
2   a 3, 6, 9, 12, 15, 18, 21, 24, 27, 30, 33, 36
       39, 45 are in the sequence.
    b Children choose their own starting number and step.

N3.3 Multiples of 2, 5 and 10

TB page 14

A1 a 6, 10, 18, 20, 26, 30, 36, 52, 54, 60, 70, 90
    b 10, 15, 20, 25, 30, 35, 45, 55, 60, 70, 90, 95
    c 10, 20, 30, 60, 70, 90

A2 a 175, 160, 195, 105
    b 122, 164, 178, 106, 152
    c 190, 170, 130, 200

B1 a 170
    b 190
    c 130

B2 Any machine with even numbers only in it.

N3.4 Multiples of 50 and 100

TB page 15

A1 a 50   b 250   c 400
    d 600   e 750   f 1000

A2 3 of 350, 400, 450, 500, 550, 600, 650

B1 a 400   b 650   c 1000
    d 750   e 50

B2 Multiples of 50 end in 50 or 00.
    Multiples of 100 end in 00.
    A multiple of 100 is also a multiple of 50.
    Doubling a multiple of 50 makes a multiple of 100.
    A multiple of 50 is halfway between two multiples of 100.

C1 a 300   b 550   c 900
    d 850   e 150

N4.2 Puzzles and problems

TB page 16

★ $7 = 3 + 4$ $7 - 3 = 4$ $7 - 4 = 3$

A $9 = 4 + 3 + 2$ $9 - 4 = 3 + 2$
    $9 - 3 = 4 + 2$ $9 - 2 = 4 + 3$
    $9 - 4 - 3 = 2$ $9 - 4 - 2 = 3$
    $9 - 3 - 2 = 4$
    You may need to discuss why
    $9 = 4 + 3 + 2$ is the same as
    $4 + 3 + 2 = 9$ and $2 + 3 + 4 = 9$.

B1 There are many answers. Encourage children to look for 2 pairs with the same sum or difference. For example, with 1, 9, 4, 6 they could find:
    $1 + 9 = 4 + 6$ $9 - 6 = 4 - 1$,
    $9 - 4 = 6 - 1$ $9 - 6 + 1 = 4$,
    $9 - 4 + 1 = 6$ $6 + 4 - 9 = 1$
    $4 + 6 - 1 = 9$
    A random selection of 4 numbers gives varied numbers of equations:
    (1, 4, 5, 9)
    $1 + 4 = 5$ $5 - 4 = 1$
    $5 - 1 = 4$ $4 + 5 = 9$
    $9 - 4 = 5$ $9 - 5 = 4$
    (1, 4, 5, 10)
    $1 + 4 = 5$ $5 - 4 = 1$
    $5 - 1 = 4$ $1 + 4 + 5 = 10$
    $10 - 5 = 4 + 1$ $10 - 4 = 5 + 1$,
    $10 - 1 = 5 + 4$ $10 - 5 - 4 = 1$
    $10 - 5 - 1 = 4$ $10 - 4 - 1 = 5$

B2 For example, changing (1, 4, 5, 9) to
(1, 4, 4, 9) would give:
1 + 4 + 4 = 9   9 − 4 − 4 = 1
9 − 4 − 1 = 4   9 − 4 = 4 + 1,
9 − 1 = 4 + 4

C1 Encourage children to look for a group of 3 numbers and a pair of numbers with the same sum or difference, e.g. 4, 5, 7 and 10, 6. A random selection of 5 numbers gives varied numbers of equations.

C2 Children could develop the 'What if?' question from B2 using 3 numbers the same, or extend to choosing 6 numbers.

N4.3 Grids

TB page 17

★1 a 12, 11, 11   b 9, 9, 9
    c 9, 9, 9

A1 For example:

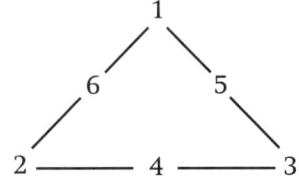

C1 Children generate their own magic triangles with 6 consecutive numbers.

N4.4 Repeating patterns

TB page 18

A1 For example:
  a There are 2 rows and 5 columns. In the rows each number is 1 greater than the number before it. A number in a column is 5 more than the number above it.
  b There are 4 rows and 3 columns. Numbers increase by 5 in rows, and by 15 in columns.
  c There are 3 rows and 6 columns. Numbers decrease by 3 in the rows and by 1 in the columns.

B1 Children generate their own patterns on CM 12.

CM 11

1 2   4   6   8   10
   12 14 16 **18** 20
   Numbers go up by 2 in the rows.
   Numbers go up by 10 in the columns.

2 5   **10** 15 20 25
   30 35 **40** 45 50
   55 **60** 65 **70** 75
   Numbers go up by 5 in the rows.
   Numbers go up by 25 in the columns.

3 3   4   5
   6   7   8
   9   10 11
   12 13 14
   Numbers go up by 1 in the rows.
   Numbers go up by 3 in the columns.

N4.5 Extending patterns

TB pages 19–20

A1 a 51, 53, 55, 57, 59
       b 78, 80, 82, 84

B1 a For example:
          2, 6, 10, 14, 18, …   20, 24, 28, 32, 36, …
       b 58, 63, 68, 73, 78

B2 a Steps of 2, 4, 5 and 10 will land exactly on 100
       b 47, 49, 51, 53, 55, 57
          47, 51, 55, 59, 63, 67

CM 14

1 a 27, 29, 31, 33, 35, 37, 39
   b 27, 31, 35, 39, 43, 47, 51
   c The numbers 27, 31, 35, 39 are in both jump patterns.

2 30, 35, 40, 45, 50, 55, 60

3 7, 12, 17, 22, 27, 32, 37
   62, 67, 72, 77, 82, 87, 92
   The jumps are 5s.
   All the numbers end in 2 or 7.

Place value

PV1.1 Introducing hundreds

TB pages 21–22

B1 a seventy-four
    b one hundred and seven
    c two hundred and sixty-five
    d three hundred and eighty-three
    e four hundred and fifty

B2 a The digit 4 represents 4 hundreds
    b The digit 4 represents 4 tens
    c The digit 4 represents 4 units

B3 a 275 = 200 + 70 + 5
    b 492 = 400 + 90 + 2
    c 316 = 300 + 10 + 6
    d 108 = 100 + 8

B4 a 341, 357 or 379
    b 471
    c 260
    d 86, 124, 165 or 174

C1 a 523 = 500 + 20 + 3
    b 442 = 400 + 40 + 2
    c 334 = 300 + 30 + 4

CM 15

1   287   two hundr...
    224   2 hu...
    365

2   5.
    75p
    125p   2 × 10p   5 × 1p
    241   £1   4 × 10p   1 × 1p

PV1.2 Changing hundreds

TB page 23

C1 208, 217, 226, 235, 244, 253, 262, 271, 280

C2 109, 118, 127, 136, 145, 154, 163, 172, 181, 190
    307, 316, 325, 334, 343, 352, 361, 370
    406, 415, 424, 433, 442, 451, 460
    505, 514, 523, 532, 541, 550
    604, 613, 622, 631, 640, and so on

C3 If you had 20 counters and used all of them each time you could make:
    299, 389, 398, 479, 488, 497, 569, 578, 587, 596, 659, 668, 676, 686, 695, 749, 758, 767, 776, 785, 794, 839, 848, 857, 867, 875, 884, 893, 929, 938, 947, 956, 965, 974, 983, 992

CM 16

1   220   230   330   340   350
    270   280   290   300   400
    250   350   360   460   470

2   200 + 200 = 400
    190 + 210 = 400
    180 + 220 = 400
    170 + 230 = 400
    160 + 240 = 400
    150 + 250 = 400
    140 + 260 = 400
    130 + 270 = 400
    120 + 280 = 400
    110 + 290 = 400
    100 + 300 = 400

3   10 less   100 less
    417 → 407   417 → 317
    339 → 329   339 → 239
    206 → 196   296 → 196

Comparing numbers

24–25

5, 133, 139, 201, 275, 382, 416

The missing numbers could be:
131 or 132; 134, 135 or 136; 135, 136 or 137; 136, 137 or 138

B1 a 12th is a tennis ball.
    b 16th is a cricket ball.
    c 3, 6, 9, 12, 15, 18, 21, 24
    d 27th is a tennis ball, 29th is a cricket ball.

C1 [hundred square grid with circled numbers: 3, 6, 9, 12, 15, 18, 21, 24, 27, 30, 33, 36, 39, 42, 45, 48, 51, 54, 57, 60, 63, 66, 69, 72, 75, 78, 81, 84, 87, 90, 93, 96, 99]

CM 18

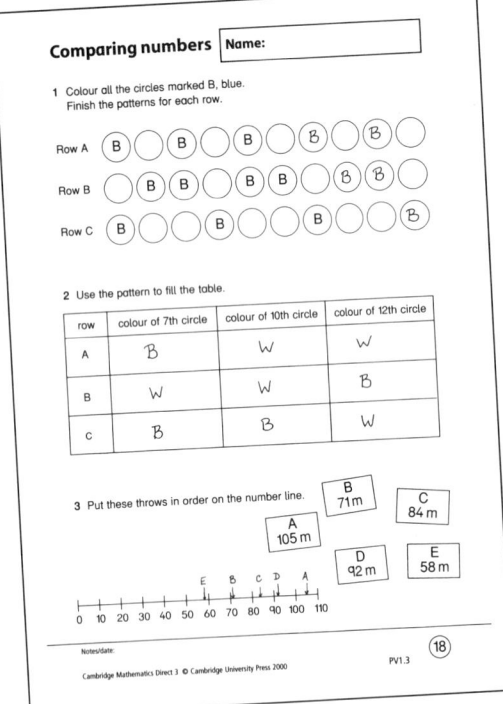

PV2.1 Investigating 3-digit numbers

TB pages 26–28

A1 a 532 235
   b 984 489
   c 761 167
   d 853 358
   e 997 799

A2 a 532 = 500 + 30 + 2
     235 = 200 + 30 + 5
   b 984 = 900 + 80 + 4
     489 = 400 + 80 + 9
   c 761 = 700 + 60 + 1
     167 = 100 + 60 + 7
   d 853 = 800 + 50 + 3
     358 = 300 + 50 + 8
   e 997 = 900 + 90 + 7
     799 = 700 + 90 + 9

B1 a Two out of 407, 470, 704, 740
   b Two out of 306, 630, 603, 630

B2 0 tens: 505, 506, 606 (from smallest to largest)
   0 units: 560, 640, 650 (from smallest to largest)

C1 147, 174, 417, 471, 714, 741

C2 The largest number is 741
   The smallest number is 147
   The number nearest 500 is 471
   The odd numbers are 147, 417, 471, 741

C3 111, 114, 117, 141, 147, 171, 174, 411, 417, 471, 711, 714, 741

PV2.2 Adding and subtracting 1, 10 or 100

TB pages 29–30

B1 a 260, 270, 280, 290, 300, 310
   b 904, 903, 902, 901, 900, 899
   c 430, 530, 630, 730, 830, 930

B2 a 149 b 166 c 157 d 178 e 179

B3 a

number	−1	−10	−100
390	389	379	279
391	390	380	280
401	400	390	290
411	410	400	300

   b When you subtract 10 or 100 the units stay the same.
     When you subtract 100 the tens digit stays the same.
     When you subtract 111, numbers with 1 in the units place end up with zero units.

C1 a £9.41   b £9.39   c £9.50
   d £9.30   e £10.40 f £8.40

C2 £2

CM 19

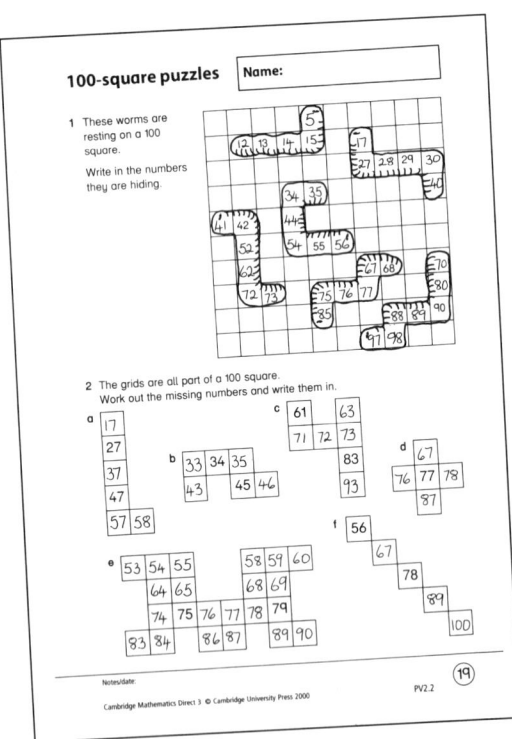

PV2.3 Numbers between

TB page 31

★1 a 560 g b £8.50 c 175 m d 216 km
   e 5.3 kg f 10.4 kg g 630p h 989 m

B1 a 17 kg, 18 kg or 19 kg
   b any length between 70 m and 80 m
   c any price from £8.01 to £8.99
   d any whole number of metres from 81 to 119

B2 any weight between 13 kg and 14 kg, e.g. 13.5 kg

CM 20

1 a 60
   b 450
   c 85
   d 670
   e 430

2 a 218, 220, 222, 224
   b 890, 892, 894, 896
   c 507, 509, 511, 513
   d 139, 141, 143, 145

3 The numbers in rows 2a and b are even. The numbers in rows 2c and d are odd.

PV3.1 Ordering whole numbers

TB pages 32–33

A1 a three hundred and twenty-four
   b four hundred and nineteen
   c 5 hundreds, 5 tens, 4 units
   d six hundred and eighty
   e 7 hundreds, 6 tens, 4 units

A2 401, 406, 410, 416, 461

A3 a 100 + 30 + 7 = 137
   b 500 + 80 + 6 = 586
   c 600 + 90 + 0 = 690
   d 900 + 0 + 3 = 903

B1 a 365 = 300 + 60 + 5
   b 217 = 200 + 10 + 7
   c 535 = 500 + 30 + 5
   d 877 = 800 + 70 + 7

B2 360   251   633

C Children generate their own puzzle

CM 21

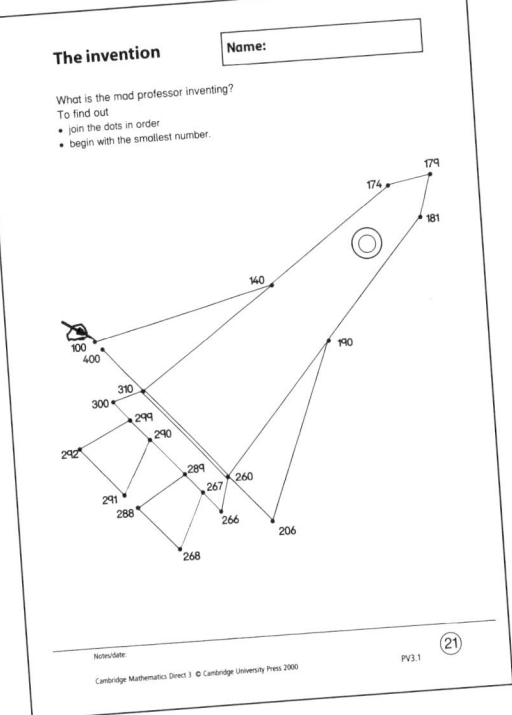

PV 3.2 Comparing

TB pages 34–35

B1

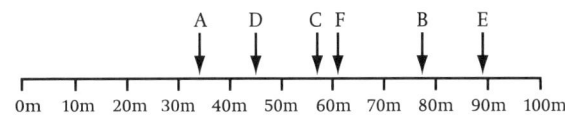

B2 a B and E   b A and D   c C and F
   d E   e F   f D
   g B

CM 22

1 401, 406, 410, 416, 460

2 248 g, **249 g**, **250 g**, 251 g, 252 g, **253 g**

3 a 623, **624**, **625**, **626**, 627
      The largest is 627.
   b **399**, **302**, 250, **241**, 236
      The smallest is 236.
   c 100 g, **150 g**, **250 g**, 500 g
      The heaviest is 500 g.
   d 99 cm, **1 m 5 cm**, **1 m 50 cm**, 2 m
      The shortest is 99 cm.

PV3.3 Reading scales
TB pages 36–37

B1 a 300 grams   b 600 grams
    c 100 grams   d 800 grams

B2 There are no units shown on the gauge. This could be a point for discussion in the Plenary
    a 45, 80   b 35

B3 35

B4 A 54 °C   B 60 °C   C 81 °C
    D 82 °C   E 8 °C

CM 23

1 30 °C, 10 °C, 0 °C, 100 °C, 20 °C

2 Check that the levels drawn match the temperatures given.

Rounding

R1.2 Number lines
TB pages 38–39

A1 a 10, 15, 18   b 39, 41, 44
    c 50, 70, 90   d 20, 30, 40, 80

B1

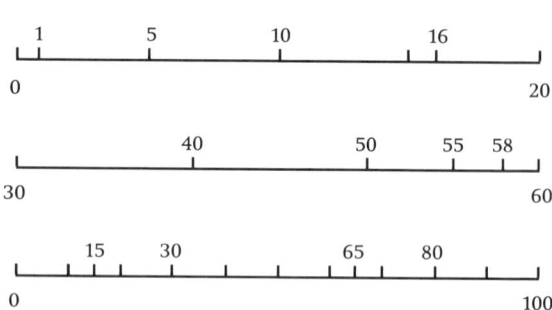

C1

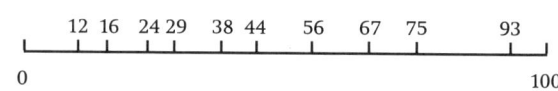

CM 26

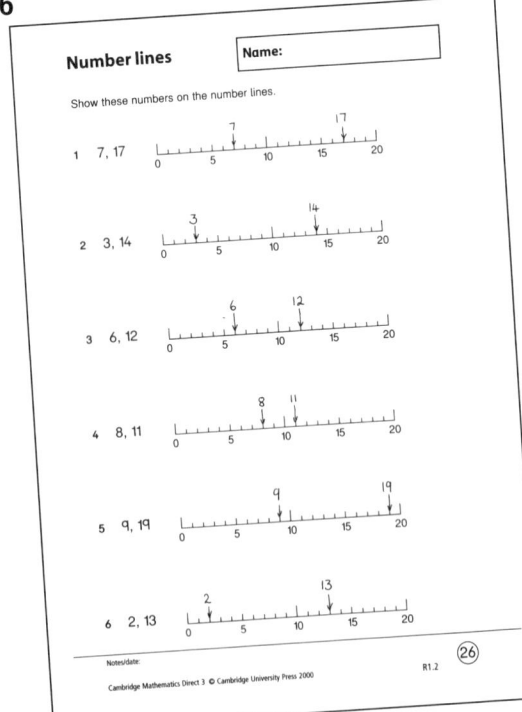

R1.3 Rounding to 10 and 100

TB pages 40–41

★1 a 10   b 20   c 10
    d 20   e 20   f 10
    g 20   h 20

★2 a 15   b 14

A1 a 65, 71, 72 round to 70. 79 rounds to 80
    b 7, 11, 14 round to 10. 18 rounds to 20
    c 48, 53, 54 round to 50. 42 rounds to 40
    d 36, 41, 44 round to 40. 48 rounds to 50

A2 a 66, 67, 68, 69, 73 or 74
    b 5, 6, 8, 9, 12 or 13
    c 45, 46, 47, 49, 51 or 52
    d 35, 37, 38, 39, 42 or 43

A3 a 200   b 500   c 800
    d 300   e 100

A4 Children's choice of numbers

B1 65, 66, 67, 68, 69, 71, 72, 73, 74

B2 Any 20 numbers between 250 and 349

C1 The numbers that round to 10 are 5–14
    The numbers that round to 20 are 15–24
    The numbers that round to 30 are 25–34,
    and so on
    d The numbers that round to a tens
       number are all numbers from 5 less
       than the tens number to 4 more than it.

Fractions

F1.1 Fractions of shapes

TB page 42

A1 a $\frac{1}{4}$ b $\frac{1}{2}$ c $\frac{1}{3}$
    d $\frac{1}{2}$ e $\frac{1}{5}$ f $\frac{1}{10}$

A2 a 4   b 2   c 3
    d 2   e 5   f 10

B1 Check that each shape has been divided into equal parts.

B2 $\frac{1}{6}$

C1 Children's own fraction puzzles

F1.2 Equal and unequal

TB page 43

A1 b and c

A2 b and d

A3 a, c and d

B1 For example:

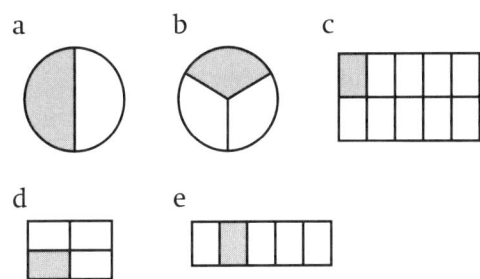

B2 For example:

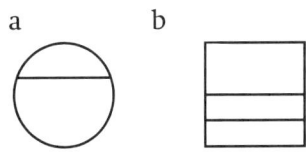

F1.3 Fractions of a set

TB pages 44–45

★1 3

★2 2

★3 1

A1 a 5   b 3   c 1

A2 a 12 b 8   c 6   d 4   e 2   f 1

B1 $\frac{1}{2}$

B2 a $\frac{1}{3}$ b $\frac{1}{5}$

B3 For example: Half of 18 is 9. Half of 16 is 8. Half of 8 is 4. Half of 6 is 3.

C1 For example: One fifth have red hair.

F1.4 Further fractions of a set

TB pages 46–47

A1 $1 \to \frac{1}{2}$ $2 \to 1$ $3 \to 1\frac{1}{2}$
    $4 \to 2$ $5 \to 2\frac{1}{2}$ $6 \to 3$
    $7 \to 3\frac{1}{2}$ $8 \to 4$ $9 \to 4\frac{1}{2}$
    $10 \to 5$ $11 \to 5\frac{1}{2}$ $12 \to 6$
    $13 \to 6\frac{1}{2}$ $14 \to 7$ $15 \to 7\frac{1}{2}$
    $16 \to 8$ $17 \to 8\frac{1}{2}$ $18 \to 9$
    $19 \to 9\frac{1}{2}$ $20 \to 10$ $21 \to 10\frac{1}{2}$
    $22 \to 11$ $23 \to 11\frac{1}{2}$ $24 \to 12$
    $25 \to 12\frac{1}{2}$ $26 \to 13$ $27 \to 13\frac{1}{2}$
    $28 \to 14$ $29 \to 14\frac{1}{2}$ $30 \to 15$

B1 $2\frac{1}{3}$

B2 $3\frac{1}{4}$

B3 $4\frac{1}{5}$

C1 Half of 30 is 15
    Half of 15 is $7\frac{1}{2}$

C2 Children halve other numbers.
    All the odd numbers take 1 step to reach an answer with a $\frac{1}{2}$ in it.
    Even numbers take between 2 and 5 steps.

F1.5 Simple fraction problems

TB page 48

B1 a 2 white   b 2 brown
    c 4 pink and 5 yellow

B2 2 green cubes, 4 blue cubes, 6 red cubes

C1 a 5 rabbits are white.
    b 6 cats are ginger.
    c $\frac{1}{5}$ of my sweets are sherbet.
    d I have 20 apples.

C2 Children generate their own fraction problems.

CM 29

Children should show:
2 people wearing boots
6 with brown hair
3 with blue eyes
4 wearing a scarf
6 wearing a hat

F2.1 Thirds

TB pages 49–50

★1 a yes   b no   c no
    d yes   e no   f yes

A1 a $\frac{2}{3}$ b $\frac{2}{3}$ c $\frac{1}{3}$
    d $\frac{2}{3}$ e $\frac{2}{3}$

A2 a 4   b 8

B1 Children should have drawn on CM 30:
    6 bow ties, 12 hats, 12 ice-creams, 6 with a flake, and 12 red noses.

C1 a 6 cakes   b $\frac{1}{3}$

C2 a 12 cakes   b $\frac{2}{3}$

C3 a 8   b $\frac{1}{3}$

C4 $\frac{1}{3}$

C5 $\frac{2}{3}$

C6 6 cakes

C7 8 sweets

F2.2 Halves and quarters

TB pages 51–52

A1 a half   b half
    c yes, half is shaded

A2 a $\frac{3}{4}$ b $\frac{1}{4}$
    c no, half is not shaded

A3 a $\frac{1}{4}$ b $\frac{3}{4}$
    c no, half is not shaded

A4 Child's square with half blue and half red

B1 a $\frac{1}{4}$ b $\frac{1}{2}$ c $\frac{1}{2}$

B2 a 18 have itchy feet.
    b 12 have helmets.
    c 12 wear wigs.
    d The same number wear wigs as wear helmets.

C   Children's alien with $\frac{3}{4}$ of its arms green, $\frac{1}{2}$ of its eyes orange and $\frac{1}{2}$ of its feet hairy

CM 31

1 2 blue triangles and 2 green triangles

2 None of the cake is left

3 Children draw a bee on 4 flowers and a butterfly on 4 flowers.

F2.3 Tenths

TB pages 53–54

A1　a　Sharmi $\frac{3}{10}$　Robert $\frac{5}{10}$ or $\frac{1}{2}$
　　　　Claire $\frac{4}{10}$ or $\frac{2}{5}$
　　b　Robert's shape is half shaded.
　　c　Robert has coloured 5 tenths.

A2　a　3 inside, 7 outside
　　b　5 inside, 5 outside
　　c　6 inside, 4 outside
　　d　2 inside, 8 outside
　　e　8 inside, 2 outside
　　f　5 inside, 5 outside

B1　Children's own cube shapes, with 10 cubes one colour, 4 cubes another colour, and 6 cubes a third colour

C1　a　3　　b　1　　c　0
　　d　3　　e　2

F2.4 Fractions of shapes

TB page 55

A1　a　$\frac{1}{6}$
　　b　Five sixths and one sixth make one whole.

A2　a　$\frac{3}{10}$
　　b　Seven tenths and three tenths make one whole.

A3　a　$\frac{1}{3}$
　　b　Two thirds and one third make one whole.

A4　a　$\frac{2}{8}$
　　b　Six eighths and two eighths make one whole.

A5　a　$\frac{3}{6}$
　　b　Three sixths and three sixths make one whole.
　　c　One half and one half make one whole.

CM 35

1　$\frac{3}{4}$ is white.　One quarter and three quarters make one whole.
2　$\frac{3}{5}$ is white.　Two fifths and three fifths make one whole.
3　$\frac{7}{10}$ is white.　Three tenths and seven tenths make one whole.

F2.5 More fractions of sets

TB page 56

B1

15	$\frac{1}{5}$	$\frac{2}{5}$	$\frac{3}{5}$	$\frac{4}{5}$	$\frac{5}{5}$
	3	6	9	12	15

12	$\frac{1}{3}$	$\frac{2}{3}$	$\frac{3}{3}$
	4	8	12

14	$\frac{1}{7}$	$\frac{2}{7}$	$\frac{3}{7}$	$\frac{4}{7}$	$\frac{5}{7}$	$\frac{6}{7}$	$\frac{7}{7}$
	2	4	6	8	10	12	14

C1　a　One third is 10, two thirds is 20 and three thirds is 30.
　　b　One fifth is 6, two fifths is 12, three fifths is 18, four fifths is 24, five fifths is 30.
　　c　One tenth is 3, two tenths is 6, … ten tenths is 30.
　　d　Half is 15, two halves is 30.

C2　$\frac{1}{5}$ and $\frac{2}{10}$ are equivalent.
　　$\frac{2}{5}$ and $\frac{4}{10}$ are equivalent.
　　$\frac{3}{5}$ and $\frac{6}{10}$ are equivalent.
　　$\frac{4}{5}$ and $\frac{8}{10}$ are equivalent.
　　$\frac{1}{2}$ and $\frac{5}{10}$ are equivalent.
　　$\frac{2}{2}, \frac{3}{3}, \frac{5}{5},$ and $\frac{10}{10}$ are equivalent.

CM 37

Number in the set	$\frac{1}{4}$	$\frac{2}{4}$	$\frac{3}{4}$	$\frac{4}{4}$	$\frac{1}{2}$	1
4	1	2	3	4	2	4
8	2	4	6	8	4	8
12	3	6	9	12	6	12
16	4	8	12	16	8	16
20	5	10	15	20	10	20
24	6	12	18	24	12	24
28	7	14	21	28	14	28

F3.1　0–1 number line　CM 38

TB page 57

★1　a quarter
A1　Check that each shape has been divided into equal parts.
A2　a　$\frac{1}{4}$　　　　　　　　b　$\frac{3}{4}$
B1　a　12 → 6 → 3　　$\frac{1}{4}$ of 12 is 3
　　b　24 → 12 → 6　　$\frac{1}{4}$ of 24 is 6
　　c　40 → 20 → 10　　$\frac{1}{4}$ of 40 is 10
　　d　18 → 9 → $4\frac{1}{2}$　　$\frac{1}{4}$ of 18 is $4\frac{1}{2}$
　　e　16 → 8 → 4　　$\frac{1}{4}$ of 16 is 4
　　f　8 → 4 → 2　　$\frac{1}{4}$ of 8 is 2

g $4 \to 2 \to 1$ $\frac{1}{4}$ of 4 is 1
h $10 \to 5 \to 2\frac{1}{2}$ $\frac{1}{4}$ of 10 is $2\frac{1}{2}$
i $80 \to 40 \to 20$ $\frac{1}{4}$ of 80 is 20
j $60 \to 30 \to 15$ $\frac{1}{4}$ of 60 is 15

F3.2 Number line to 10 (quarters)

TB page 58

B1 a $3\frac{1}{2}$ b $2\frac{3}{4}$ c $3\frac{1}{4}$

B2 a $6\frac{1}{2}$ b $7\frac{1}{4}$ c $6\frac{3}{4}$

B3 a $\frac{3}{4}$ b 2   c $\frac{3}{4}$

C1 Children's number line and questions

CM 40

1 Halves marked in red

2 Quarters marked in green

3 Halves marked in red and green, other quarters in green
   The half number marks are both red and green.
   Some quarter numbers are also half numbers.

F3.3 Tenths on a number line

TB pages 59–60

B1 a $\frac{2}{10}$ b $\frac{4}{10}$ c $\frac{5}{10}$
    d $\frac{7}{10}$ e $\frac{9}{10}$

B2 $\frac{5}{10}$ and $\frac{6}{10}$ Children might also say $\frac{1}{2}$ and $\frac{3}{5}$

B3 Any of $\frac{1}{2}, \frac{5}{10}, \frac{2}{5}, \frac{4}{10}$

C1 a $3\frac{6}{10}, 3\frac{7}{10}, 3\frac{8}{10}$ or $3\frac{9}{10}$
    b $2\frac{1}{10}, 2\frac{2}{10}, 2\frac{3}{10}$ or $2\frac{4}{10}$
    c $3\frac{1}{10}, 3\frac{2}{10}, 3\frac{3}{10}$ or $3\frac{4}{10}$

C2 a $7\frac{6}{10}, 7\frac{7}{10}, 7\frac{8}{10}, 7\frac{9}{10}, 8, 8\frac{1}{10}, 8\frac{2}{10}, 8\frac{3}{10}$ or $8\frac{4}{10}$
    b $7\frac{2}{10}, 7\frac{3}{10}$ or $7\frac{4}{10}$
    c $8\frac{1}{10}, 8\frac{2}{10}, 8\frac{3}{10}, 8\frac{4}{10}, 8\frac{5}{10}, 8\frac{6}{10}, 8\frac{7}{10}, 8\frac{8}{10}$ or $8\frac{9}{10}$

C3 a $\frac{1}{10}, \frac{2}{10}, \frac{3}{10}$ or $\frac{4}{10}$
    b $1, 1\frac{1}{10}, 1\frac{2}{10}, 1\frac{3}{10}$ or $1\frac{4}{10}$
    c $1\frac{6}{10}, 1\frac{7}{10}, 1\frac{8}{10}$ or $1\frac{9}{10}$

CM 41

1	3 squares coloured	$\frac{3}{10}$ is **less** than $\frac{1}{2}$
2	9 squares coloured	$\frac{9}{10}$ is **more** than $\frac{1}{2}$
3	6 squares coloured	$\frac{6}{10}$ is **more** than $\frac{1}{2}$
4	1 square coloured	$\frac{1}{10}$ is **less** than $\frac{1}{2}$
5	8 squares coloured	$\frac{8}{10}$ is **more** than $\frac{1}{2}$

F3.4 Estimating fractions

TB page 61

B1 a nearly 3 o'clock   b about half past 11
    c about quarter past 7

B2 a about 25   b about 10

B3

C1 Children's own estimating fractions questions

CM 42

1 & 2 Check that levels coloured are correct.

3 Check that levels coloured match children's choices of fraction.

F3.5 Fraction patterns

TB pages 62–63

★1 a The numbers increase by $\frac{1}{2}$. The first number is 0.
    b The next number will be $2\frac{1}{2}$

★2 a The numbers increase by $\frac{1}{4}$. The first number is 0.
    b The next number will be $1\frac{2}{4}$

A1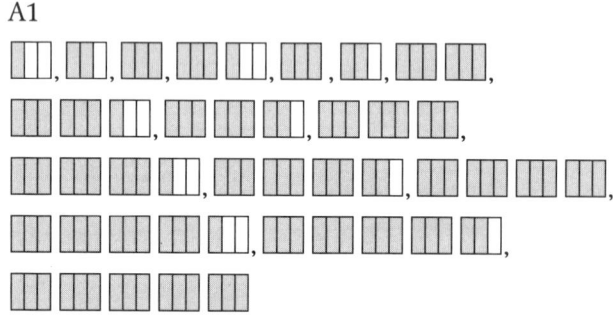

A2 $\frac{2}{3}, 1\frac{1}{3}, 2, 2\frac{2}{3}, 3\frac{1}{3}, 4, 4\frac{2}{3}, 5\frac{1}{3}, 6$

A3 a $\frac{3}{10}$ b $\frac{5}{10}$ c $\frac{5}{10}$

A4 a Flag with 10 spaces, 3 red, 5 blue, 2 yellow
    b Flag with 10 spaces, 1 yellow, 8 blue, 1 red
    c Flag with 10 triangles, 2 each yellow, red, blue, green and white

B1 For example:
    2 halves make 1 whole
    4 halves make 2 wholes
    6 halves make 3 wholes

B2 Odd numbers of halves make a whole number and a half. For example:
3 halves make $1\frac{1}{2}$
5 halves make $2\frac{1}{2}$
7 halves make $3\frac{1}{2}$

CM 43

C1 For example:
  a 3 quarters is a quarter less than one whole.
  b 7 quarters is a quarter less than 2
     9 quarters is a quarter more than 2

C2 a $1 \times 10 = 10$ $\frac{10}{10} = 1$
    b $2 \times 10 = 20$ $\frac{20}{10} = 2$
    c $4 \times 10 = 40$ $\frac{40}{10} = 4$

C3 a $\frac{1}{3} \times 3 = 1$
    b $\frac{1}{3} \times 6 = 2$
    c $\frac{1}{3} \times 12 = 4$

C4 Children's own statement and examples.

Assessment

CM 46   What's my rule?

1   4, 9, 14, 19, **24**, **29**, 34
2   3, 7, 11, **15**, **19**, **23**, 27
3   2, 5, 8, **11**, **14**, **17**, 20
4   1, 6, 11, **16**, **21**, **26**, 31
5   5, 9, 13, **17**, **21**, **25**, **29**
6   6, 16, 26, **36**, **46**, **56**, **66**
7   Children generate their own sequence for a friend to complete.

CM 47   The number cruncher

1   a 26
    b 48
    c 140
    d 62
    e 216
    f 454

2   a 15
    b 37
    c 91
    d 189
    e 668

3   a The machine is adding 100.
    b 193
    c 345
    d 561
    e 999

CM 48   Estimating and rounding

2   Numbers rounding to 10: 5, 7, 12, 13, 14
    Numbers rounding to 20: 16, 24, 19

3   34 is in the wrong set. It rounds to 30 not 40.
    Children could add:
    26, 28, 29, 32 or 34 to the set that rounds to 30
    35, 36, 38, 39, 42 or 43 to the set that rounds to 40.

CM 49 Find the fraction

1, 2, 3 Children shade fractions of the shapes

4   2 beetles coloured green

5   3 butterflies coloured red

6   2 have blue eyes.

7   2 biscuits are choc-chip.

CM 50 Fractions of shapes

1   b

2   d

3   c

4   1a $\frac{2}{3}$, 1b $\frac{1}{2}$, 1c $\frac{2}{3}$
         2a $\frac{2}{5}$, 2b $\frac{1}{2}$, 2d $\frac{3}{4}$
         3a $\frac{3}{4}$, 3c $\frac{2}{3}$, 3d $\frac{2}{4}$ or $\frac{1}{2}$

CM 51 Ordering fractions

1   a $\frac{2}{10}$ $\frac{5}{10}$ $\frac{6}{10}$
        b   8 $8\frac{1}{10}$ $8\frac{9}{10}$
        c $4\frac{4}{10}$ $4\frac{1}{2}$ $4\frac{7}{10}$
        d $5\frac{1}{2}$ $5\frac{9}{10}$ 6

2   Any one of:
        a $3\frac{6}{10}$ $3\frac{7}{10}$ $3\frac{8}{10}$ $3\frac{9}{10}$ $3\frac{3}{5}$ $3\frac{4}{5}$ $3\frac{2}{3}$ $3\frac{3}{4}$
        b $\frac{1}{10}$ $\frac{2}{10}$ $\frac{1}{5}$ $\frac{1}{4}$
        c $\frac{6}{10}$ $\frac{7}{10}$ $\frac{8}{10}$ $\frac{9}{10}$ $\frac{3}{5}$ $\frac{4}{5}$ $\frac{2}{3}$ $\frac{3}{4}$
        d $2\frac{9}{10}$ $2\frac{8}{10}$ $2\frac{7}{10}$ $2\frac{6}{10}$ $2\frac{4}{5}$ $2\frac{3}{5}$ $2\frac{2}{3}$ $2\frac{3}{4}$
        e $9\frac{9}{10}$ $9\frac{8}{10}$ $9\frac{7}{10}$ $9\frac{6}{10}$ $9\frac{4}{5}$ $9\frac{3}{5}$ $9\frac{2}{3}$ $9\frac{3}{4}$
        f $\frac{1}{2}$ $\frac{5}{10}$ $\frac{6}{10}$ $\frac{7}{10}$ $\frac{3}{5}$ $\frac{2}{3}$ $\frac{3}{4}$
        g $6\frac{4}{10}$ $6\frac{3}{10}$ $6\frac{2}{10}$ $6\frac{2}{5}$ $6\frac{1}{5}$ $6\frac{1}{3}$ $6\frac{1}{4}$
        h $9\frac{1}{10}$ $9\frac{2}{10}$ $9\frac{3}{10}$ $9\frac{4}{10}$ $9\frac{1}{5}$ $9\frac{2}{5}$ $9\frac{1}{4}$ $9\frac{1}{3}$